MIXED MARTIAL ARTS

MMA: TARGETED TRAINING

Frazer Andrew Krohn

Abdo & Daughters
MIDDLE GRADE NONFICTION
An imprint of Abdo Publishing
abdobooks.com

ABDOBOOKS.COM

Published by Abdo Publishing, a division of ABDO, PO Box 398166, Minneapolis, Minnesota 55439. Copyright © 2023 by Abdo Consulting Group, Inc. International copyrights reserved in all countries. No part of this book may be reproduced in any form without written permission from the publisher. Abdo & Daughters™ is a trademark and logo of Abdo Publishing.

102022
012023

THIS BOOK CONTAINS RECYCLED MATERIALS

Design: Kelly Doudna, Mighty Media, Inc.
Production: Mighty Media, Inc.
Editor: Liz Salzmann
Cover Photograph: Louis Grasse/PxImages/Icon Sportswire/AP Images
Interior Photographs: A.RICARDO/Shutterstock Images, pp. 15, 22–23, 55 (left), 60 (bottom left); Ahturner/Shutterstock Images, p. 11; Ajan Alen/Shutterstock Images, pp. 8–9; Andre Luiz Moreira/Shutterstock Images, pp. 26, 40 (top), 42 (left), 44 (bottom), 50 (bottom); antoniodiaz/Shutterstock Images, pp. 30–31; Boris Riaposov/Shutterstock Images, p. 20 (top); Carlos Montoya/Shutterstock Images, p. 43 (right); Cassiano Correia/Shutterstock Images, pp. 27, 42 (right), 46 (top), 50 (top), 51; Corey Sipkin/AP Images, p. 24; Darren Calabrese/AP Images, pp. 48–49, 60 (top); Dawid S Swierczek/Shutterstock Images, pp. 47, 61 (top right); El Nariz/Shutterstock Images, p. 12 (top); George Rudy/Shutterstock Images, p. 13; imageSPACE/AP Images, p. 34; Isaac Brekken/AP Images, pp. 18, 32, 61 (top left); Jack Dempsey/AP Images, p. 44 (top left); Jacob Lund/Shutterstock Images, p. 29; John Locher/AP Images, pp. 6, 7, 54 (top), 60 (bottom right); Katherine Welles/Shutterstock Images, pp. 56–57, 61 (bottom right); Kathy Hutchins/Shutterstock Images, pp. 38 (all), 41 (top), 55 (right); L.E. BASKOW/AP Images, pp. 4–5; legendashow/Flickr, p. 43 (left); Louis Grasse/PxImages/Icon Sportswire/AP Images, pp. 33, 35, 53, 61 (bottom right); lunamarina/Shutterstock Images, p. 25; Matt Strasen/AP Images, p. 21; metamorworks/Shutterstock Images, p. 59 (top); Michael Zarrilli/AP Images, p. 46 (bottom); Miguel Discart/Wikimedia Commons, p. 54 (bottom); Nestor Rizhniak/Shutterstock Images, p. 10; Nomad_Soul/Shutterstock Images, p. 20 (bottom); oneinchpunch/Shutterstock Images, p. 14; Prostock-studio/Shutterstock Images, p. 28; Rommel Canlas/Shutterstock Images, p. 59 (bottom); UfaBizPhoto/Shutterstock Images, pp. 36–37; Vladimir Sukhachev/Shutterstock Images, p. 12 (bottom); Wikimedia Commons, pp. 16–17, 39 (all), 40 (bottom), 41 (bottom), 44 (top right), 45, 50 (middle), 52; Zuma Press, Inc./Alamy Photo, p. 58
Design Elements: Mighty Media, Inc.; mkirarslan/iStockphoto; sanchesnet1/iStockphoto

Library of Congress Control Number: 2022940775

Publisher's Cataloging-in-Publication Data
Names: Krohn, Frazer Andrew, author.
Title: MMA: targeted training / by Frazer Andrew Krohn
Description: Minneapolis, Minnesota : Abdo Publishing, 2023 | Series: Mixed martial arts | Includes online resources and index.
Identifiers: ISBN 9781532199240 (lib. bdg.) | ISBN 9781098274443 (ebook)
Subjects: LCSH: MMA (Mixed martial arts)--Juvenile literature. | Mixed martial arts--Juvenile literature. | Hand-to-hand fighting--Juvenile literature. | Mixed martial arts--Training--Juvenile literature. | Ultimate fighting--Juvenile literature. | Sports--History--Juvenile literature.
Classification: DDC 796.81--dc23

CONTENTS

McGregor's First Championship 5

Elements of MMA Training 9

Training Camps 17

Fighting Fitness 23

Creating a Game Plan 31

MMA Gyms 37

When Training Goes Wrong 49

The Future of MMA Training 57

Timeline 60

Glossary 62

Online Resources 63

Index 64

UFC president Dana White separates Mendes (*left*) and McGregor (*right*) during the weigh-in for their fight.

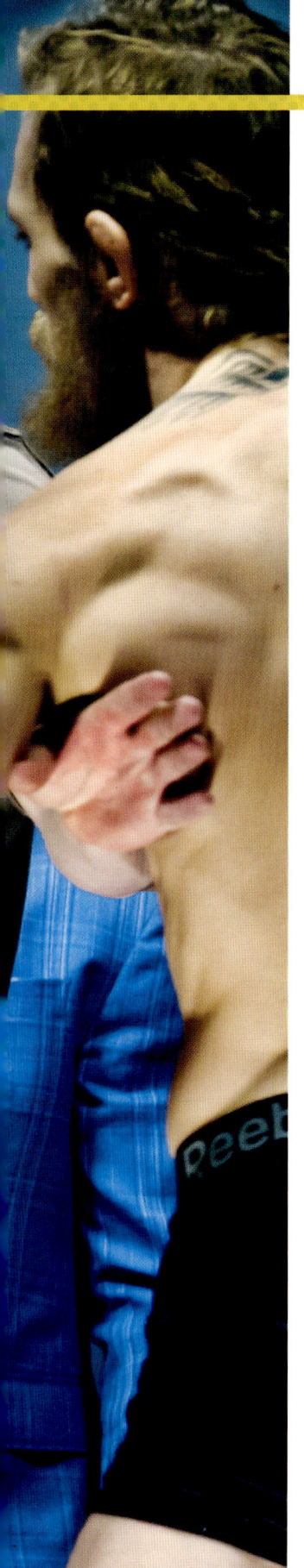

CHAPTER 1

McGREGOR'S FIRST CHAMPIONSHIP

In 2015, Conor McGregor was preparing to fight José Aldo for the Ultimate Fighting Championship (UFC) featherweight title. Aldo had held the title since November 2009. It would be McGregor's first UFC title fight. The fight would be the headliner at UFC 189 on July 11, 2015.

Not only did McGregor prepare to face Aldo in the Octagon, he also went on a 12-day press tour to hype the fight. Anticipation built among mixed martial arts (MMA) fans. As July neared, it seemed like it would be the biggest fight in UFC history. However, two weeks before the match, Aldo suffered a rib injury while training. He had to drop out of the event. Top contender Chad Mendes agreed to fight in Aldo's place.

McGregor (*left*) took out Mendes (*right*) thanks to his years of training preparing him to counter many fighting styles.

McGregor had been preparing to fight Aldo, who uses Muay Thai techniques and favors punching and leg kicks. He avoids wrestling moves. Mendes, however, is a wrestler. He always tries to take his opponents to the ground and dominate them there. So, McGregor was suddenly about to face a different style of fighting than expected. McGregor wasn't intimidated. He had trained for years and knew he had the skills to win. It was just a matter of changing his strategy.

Mendes started strong and was able to take McGregor down a few times. But each time, McGregor quickly got back on his feet and concentrated on landing strong punches and kicks. In the second round, McGregor knocked Mendes out with a powerful punch to the jaw. With that knockout, McGregor won the interim featherweight title.

McGregor's fight against Aldo was rescheduled for December 12, 2015. After another five months of training, McGregor was ready. Unfortunately for Aldo, the fight only lasted 13 seconds. McGregor landed his famous left hook, knocking Aldo out cold. McGregor was the undisputed featherweight champion. After months of training, blood, and sweat, it was over in just 13 seconds.

In December 2015, McGregor (*left*) took out Aldo (*right*) with a left-hand punch.

MMA training involves practicing moves from many different disciplines.

CHAPTER 2

ELEMENTS OF MMA TRAINING

Stepping into a cage to fight someone can be a big challenge. A fighter must be confident that they've done everything possible to prepare for that moment. That's where training comes in. A fighter goes through months of preparation for a fight that could last for just a few seconds or for 25 grueling minutes of back-and-forth action.

When getting ready for a fight, a fighter learns as much about their opponent as they can. Then they come up with a fight plan based on their own and their opponent's strengths and styles. But, as McGregor learned, fighters also have to be ready to adjust to last-minute changes.

MMA draws on multiple different martial arts including judo, jiu-jitsu, wrestling, boxing, kickboxing, and Muay Thai, among others. To be a world-class mixed martial artist, a fighter must learn elements of each of these disciplines.

JUDO AND JIU-JITSU

Judo and jiu-jitsu are the most direct precursors to MMA. They are both Japanese martial arts. Judo focuses mostly on different throwing techniques to take down opponents. Jiu-jitsu involves strikes as well as holds, submissions, and other ground techniques.

In the 1920s, several members of the Gracie family of Brazil learned judo and jiu-jitsu. They went on to combine elements of them into their own martial art, called Brazilian jiu-jitsu (BJJ). The Gracies were instrumental in developing MMA as a way to showcase BJJ.

Traditionally, judo and jiu-jitsu fighters wear *gis*. A *gi* is the loose-fitting uniform worn by many martial artists around the world. MMA fighters generally don't wear *gis* when they train or during fights. A fighter will occasionally train in a *gi* to work on specific techniques or to increase their belt level. The highest level is a black belt. Progressing from novice to black belt takes 10 to 15 years.

MMA fighters usually don't wear *gis* when training in jiu-jitsu because they don't wear them in official fights.

WRESTLING

Wrestling is seen as one of the most difficult, draining aspects of

MMA. Over the years, American and Russian fighters have been especially strong in wrestling techniques. One reason for this is that in both countries, children often learn wrestling in school. The United States in particular has a large wrestling culture, with most high schools and

Many college wrestlers, such as Ed Ruth (*front*), have gone on to fight in professional MMA promotions.

colleges offering wrestling programs. Many American MMA fighters got their start in wrestling. Wrestling training is largely about learning different holds and grappling techniques.

STRIKING

Striking is a skill used in many combat sports, such as boxing, Muay Thai, and kickboxing. Strikes include punches, kicks, and blows with the elbows and knees. There are different ways a fighter can improve their striking skills. One is working with a heavy bag. This is a large bag that is hung from the ceiling. It is usually filled with fabric, sawdust, or sand. A fighter punches and kicks the bag as if it were an opponent.

Working on a heavy bag helps a fighter increase their power and improve their technique. Since the target doesn't move, the fighter will connect more often, building strength with each blow. The heavy bag also allows a fighter to perfect striking techniques, since they don't have to worry about the target moving out of the way or hitting back. The fighter can concentrate on their own movements until they get them right consistently.

Fighters may train with their coaches using hitting pads.

Fighters can also hone their skills with striking drills. These are often conducted with a coach who is holding pads or wearing boxing gloves. Drills are different from sparring because the coach doesn't try to hit back. Instead, they hold their hands up for the fighter to hit. This allows the fighter to focus on their technique as they practice certain moves and combinations

Striking drills allow a fighter to practice a move repeatedly with a partner.

of strikes. The coach may call out certain strikes and combinations for the fighter to throw. This helps the fighter increase their coordination and reaction time.

SPARRING

Sparring is one of the main ways fighters train. Essentially, sparring is a simulated fight against a sparring partner. A fighter often tries to find a sparring partner who is about the same size as their upcoming opponent. Then the sparring partner tries to mimic the fighting style of the opponent. This gives the fighter an idea of what their opponent might do during the fight. While sparring has always been a common way to train for a fight, the ways fighters spar has changed over the years.

Training principles have progressed over time from early days to the establishment of the UFC in 1993 and on to today's MMA. Historically, it was mainly done with hard sparring. This involved

Having full-force fights to prepare for a real fight is becoming a less popular training style.

extreme workouts in the gym every day to prepare for an upcoming fight. Legendary gyms such as Brazil's Chute Boxe Academy were notorious for hard sparring that was nearly as intense and brutal as an actual fight. The idea was to practice in conditions as close to a real fight as possible.

It soon became clear that constant hard sparring wasn't the best way to train for the long term. Yes, it could help fighters see how effective their strikes and other techniques were, and they would get used to taking hits and defending themselves. However, hard sparring often caused injuries that would prevent fighters from being in fight events. And frequent injuries and high stress shortened some fighters' careers.

More recently, many fighters including McGregor have started "touch sparring." This is simulating the fight conditions, but only gently touching each other, rather than trying to knock each other out. This allows fighters to prepare in a safe manner for a fight. They can hone their timing and distance management without getting hurt. This often leads to longer, more illustrious careers, since fighters don't get hurt as often during training.

Simulating a fight with a sparring partner without hurting them is a safe and effective training method.

There are hundreds of UFC fights every year.

ULTIMATE FIGHTING CHAMPIONSHIP

The Ultimate Fighting Championship is, without a doubt, the premier MMA promotion in the world. Founded in 1993, the UFC would become the first mainstream MMA promotion. Those in the UFC had to deal with the setbacks, aid in rule progression, and be accountable for any early missteps. As the popularity of MMA grew, the UFC created more weight classes in order to make fights safer, fairer, and more competitive. Today, it's widely accepted that UFC champions are the best MMA fighters in the world.

ONE Championship's Radeem Rahman (*left*) spars at Evolve MMA in Singapore.

CHAPTER 3

TRAINING CAMPS

While MMA fighters constantly train in general techniques, they go through special programs to prepare for specific fights. These programs are called training camps. A fighter enters a training camp about 8 to 12 weeks before a fight.

During training camp, the fighter focuses on getting ready for battle, sharpening their skills and developing a game plan for defeating their upcoming opponent. A fighter spars regularly throughout the fight camp to get a feel for what their opponent may bring to the Octagon on fight night. They also practice their timing, memorize certain combinations, and work on improving their endurance.

SPARRING PARTNERS

Sparring partners are people who mimic the style of the fighter's upcoming opponent. A good sparring partner helps the fighter enter the upcoming fight confident that they won't be surprised by what their opponent has to offer. Sometimes, it can be difficult to find the right sparring partners. If a certain style isn't represented by anyone at the fighter's home gym, a sparring partner may be brought in from another gym. A fighter can also look for a sparring partner who practices a discipline other than MMA, such as wrestling or kickboxing.

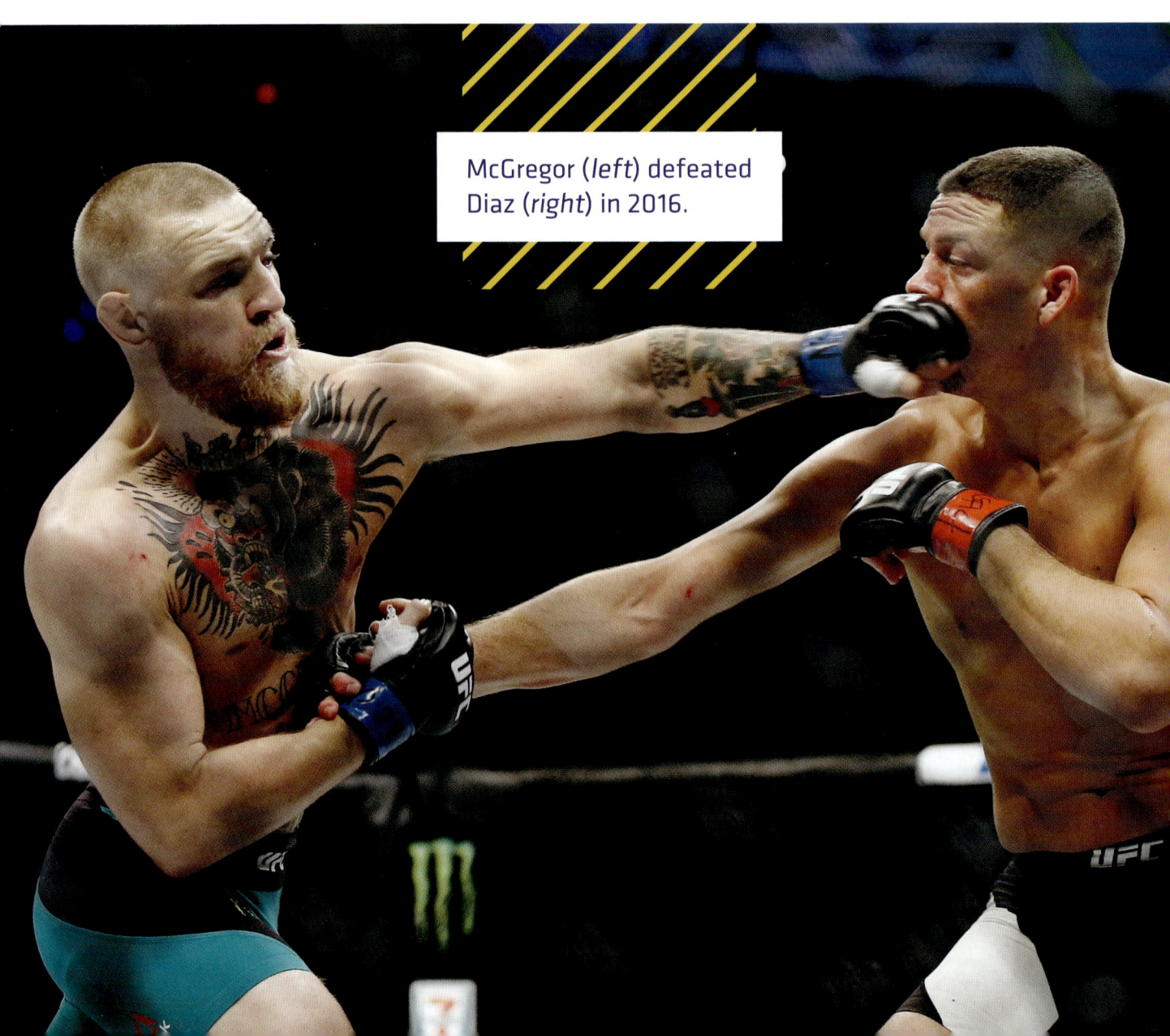

McGregor (*left*) defeated Diaz (*right*) in 2016.

An example of this is McGregor's preparation for a fight against Nate Diaz. McGregor had lost to Diaz in March 2016. A rematch was scheduled for that August. During training camp, McGregor made sure to bring in specific sparring partners to help him prepare for the rematch. One of these sparring partners was boxer Conor Wallace. Wallace was tall and left-handed and had a long reach, very similar to Diaz. The tactic worked. McGregor won the second fight against Diaz.

> **MMA ENDGAME**
>
> An MMA fight ends with either a finish or a judges' decision. A finish is when one fighter wins before the end of the rounds. This includes winning by submission, knockout, technical knockout, or disqualification. If neither fighter finishes by the end of the last round, then the winner is determined by the three fight judges. If all three judges choose the same winner, it's called a unanimous decision. If they don't all agree, it's called a split or majority decision. The winner is the fighter chosen by two of the judges.

SPARRING GOALS

Sparring isn't about winning or losing a specific round or fight. Not all sparring sessions consist of rounds like a traditional MMA fight. Often sparring sessions are designed to improve specific skills, such as getting an opponent to the ground as quickly as possible. Offensive and defensive strategies are also worked on throughout a sparring session. A session may be stopped mid-round in order for a coach to give tips or advice on how the fighter could improve.

Fighters from other sports, such as kickboxing, may spar with MMA fighters to help them train.

Sparring allows fighters to practice with a partner who copies the style of the upcoming opponent.

As previously mentioned, sparring today is rarely conducted at full intensity. When sparring, fighters aren't trying to actually knock each other out. Instead, many practice touch sparring. And some fighters, including former UFC welterweight champion Robbie Lawler, say that they no longer spar at all due to the risk of head injury. This makes sense, since no fighter wants to enter a fight injured. But not sparring may make it harder to fully prepare for an upcoming fight.

Lawler (*right*) is among the MMA fighters who don't spar in order to avoid injury.

UFC fighters like Max Holloway (*left*) and José Aldo (*right*) build their stamina so they can give their all during long fights.

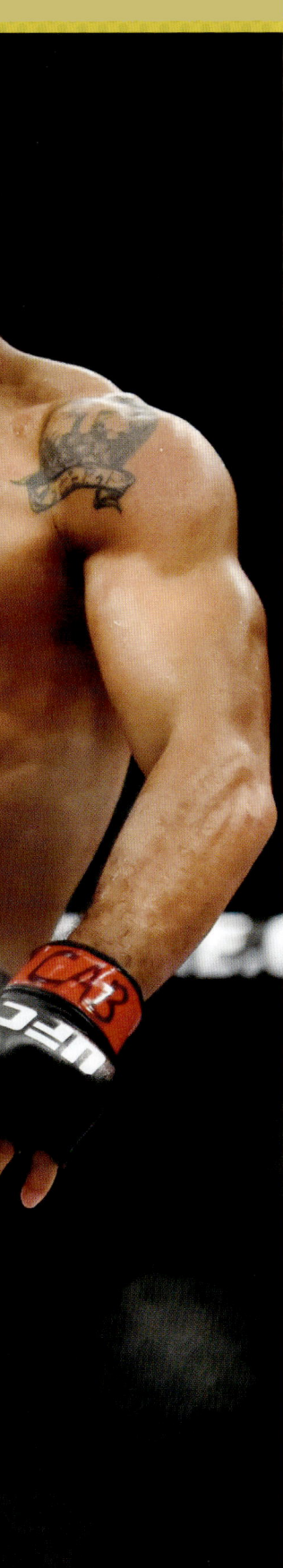

CHAPTER 4

FIGHTING FITNESS

An MMA fighter's training doesn't focus solely on improving fighting techniques. There is little point in being the best striker in the world if a fighter has poor fitness and can't last an entire fight without getting tired. Such a fighter would have to rely on getting a knockout early on. But if that doesn't happen, the fitter fighter will have the advantage.

CARDIO TRAINING

Endurance is vital to being a successful MMA fighter. The main way to improve endurance is through cardiovascular (cardio) training. Cardio workouts increase the heart rate, which strengthens the heart. This allows the body to be active longer without tiring. It's become evident, particularly in recent years, that fighters with poor cardio fitness will struggle.

Running is the traditional way fighters improve endurance. Long runs are very effective in

23

Kamaru Usman in 2021

building a fighter's cardio fitness. The risk with running, however, is that it can be hard on the body. Running is a high-impact activity, putting a lot of stress on the legs and feet. This can lead to injuries. Longtime UFC welterweight champion Kamaru Usman doesn't run during his training camps. He has a history of knee injuries, which are aggravated by running.

Today, there are anti-gravity running machines that provide cardio workouts with less stress on the body. These machines provide the cardio benefits of running while supporting the runner's weight, protecting their legs. Anti-gravity machines have become popular among MMA fighters, especially those recovering from injury.

Besides running, there are other ways MMA fighters can improve cardio fitness and endurance. These include swimming, cycling, and rowing. These are all low-impact options that increase the heart rate like running does, but they are easier on the body. Jump rope is also regularly used in fight training. It increases endurance, helps improve footwork, and speeds up reaction times.

MIGHTY MUSCLES

Cardio training improves a fighter's cardiovascular endurance. But muscle strength and conditioning are also important. MMA fighters spend a lot of time improving their strength and conditioning. MMA strength training generally focuses on improving explosive power, rather than just lifting the most weight possible.

Fighters use a variety of plyometric and ballistic exercises to build strength and power. Plyometric exercises involve repeated movements to increase muscle power. Ballistic exercises are similar to plyometric exercises but involve holding a weighted object. Common exercises used in MMA training include:

JUMP SQUATS // holding a small weight while squatting low and then jumping up as high as possible.

BOX JUMPS // jumping from the ground onto a box or bench. The height is increased over time.

MEDICINE BALL THROWS // throwing a medicine ball either against a wall or onto the floor.

KETTLEBELL SWINGS // swinging a kettlebell weight between the legs and up to chest height in a controlled manner.

MMA fighters may focus on exercises like box jumps, kettlebell swings, and more.

These and other exercises that use speed and force to build power are effective ways to increase muscle strength and conditioning. MMA fighters work with coaches and fitness experts to develop an exercise plan that will best prepare them for their upcoming fight.

WEIGHT CUTTING

UFC introduced weight classes in 1997. This means that fighters have to be within a certain weight range in order to fight. For example, a heavyweight fighter has to be between 205 and 265 pounds (93 and 120 kg). Before each fight, there is a weigh-in, where the fighters are weighed to make sure they meet the weight requirement.

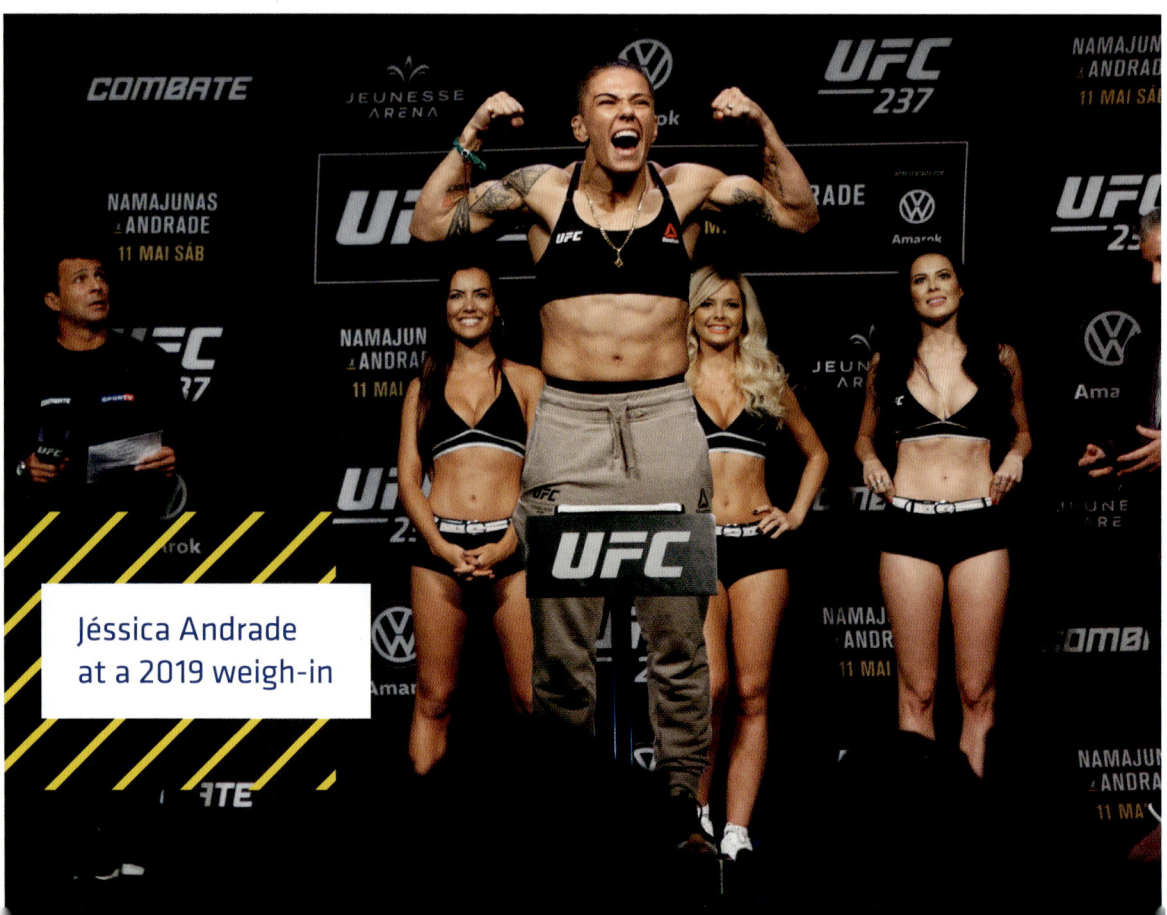

Jéssica Andrade at a 2019 weigh-in

A fighter's weight class is often lower than their usual weight. So, they need to quickly lose some weight right before a fight. Fighters commonly use a combination of dieting and weight cutting to make weight.

A fighter's training camp will include a diet plan. It's designed so they'll gradually lose weight while they are training for the fight. Dieting generally gets the fighter close to the required weight. Then about five days before weigh-in, the fighter starts reducing the amount of water they drink, and drinks little to no water the day

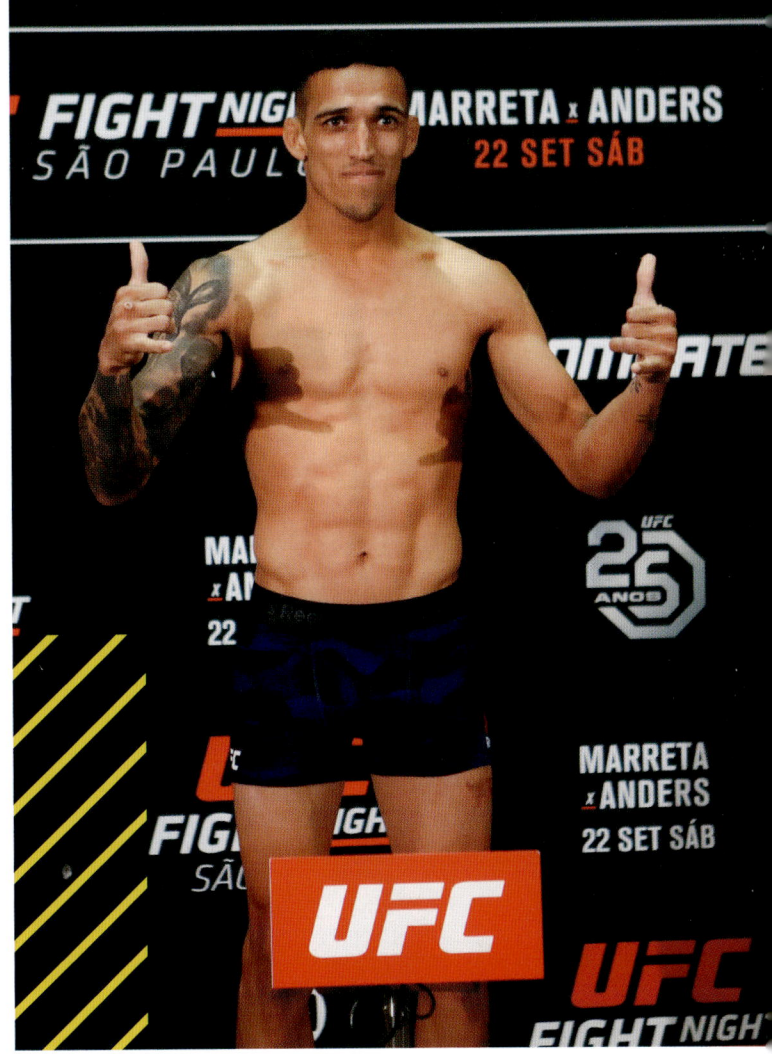

Weight cutting can be dangerous and controversial. Charles Oliveira is one fighter who was stripped of his title for missing weight.

before. They also use various methods to sweat out as much water as possible. Common methods include sitting in a sauna, taking hot baths, and working out while wearing a sweatsuit.

There is a lot of controversy over weight cutting. It's dangerous for the fighters because they are deliberately dehydrating themselves. Dehydration drains the water from the brain, which can cause dizziness and disorientation. Sometimes fighters are pulled out of a fight due to complications from weight cutting. Occasionally, fighters have been hospitalized, and some have died from dehydration.

RECOVERY

Recovery is becoming one of the most important aspects of MMA training. The faster a fighter recovers from a fight, the sooner they can start training for their next fight. There are a number of ways to recover effectively, ranging from simple methods to more advanced, technological methods.

Sleep and nutrition are key for recovery. Getting at least eight hours of sleep a night is vital to allow the body to naturally recover. It allows the body tissue to heal and promotes muscle growth. And making sure that the fighter's body is fueled with healthy, nutritious foods also aids in recovery. Most MMA fighters enhance their diets with nutrition supplements. These include vitamins and protein shakes to help the body heal and prevent muscle soreness.

Nutrition is an important aspect of training and recovery.

For many years, athletes have treated injuries and muscle aches with ice and heat. An ice pack reduces blood flow to an injured area. This helps reduce swelling and promote healing. An ice bath or cryotherapy chamber can apply extreme cold to a large area of the body, or even the whole body. Cold therapy is usually used first and is later followed by heat. Heat helps continue the recovery process by increasing blood flow and circulation. Heat helps relax injured muscles, heal damaged tissues, and improve flexibility. Sitting in a sauna is a common way to apply heat to the entire body.

Fighters work with their coaches, fitness trainers, and doctors to come up with a recovery plan after each fight. Then they can get busy training for their next match.

Athletes commonly use cryotherapy to reduce inflammation and swelling after training or competing.

Fighters and their coaches and teams work together to create specific game plans for upcoming fights.

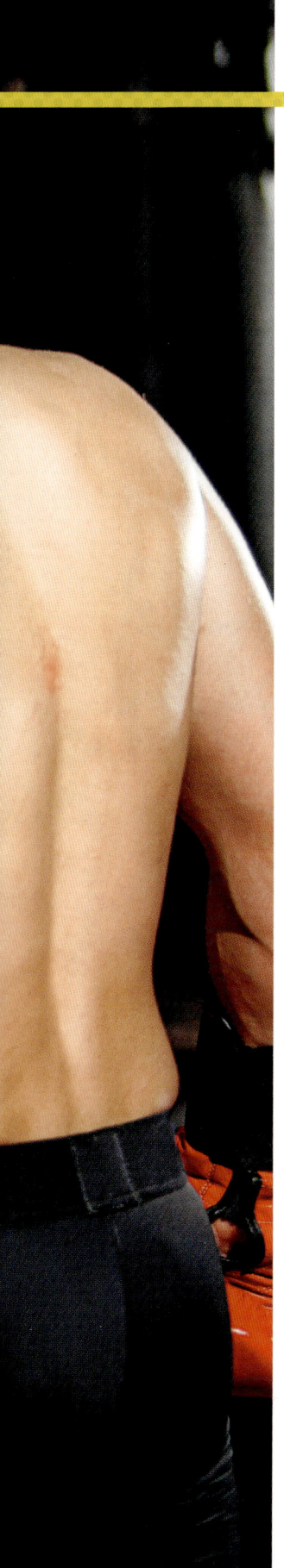

CHAPTER 5

CREATING A GAME PLAN

A fighter usually develops a game plan for each fight. The game plan outlines the fighting style, techniques, and combinations that will give the fighter the best chance at victory. The fighter works with their team to devise the game plan. The first step is watching the opponent's previous fights. They look for any weaknesses in the opponent's game that could be used to get the upper hand. Once the opponent's weaknesses are identified, the fighter's team can decide what moves and techniques could be used to exploit the weaknesses. Then they build a training camp around developing and perfecting those techniques.

Creating and successfully carrying out an effective game plan is what helps an athlete become an elite MMA fighter. The ability to implement a plan comes from the fighter's

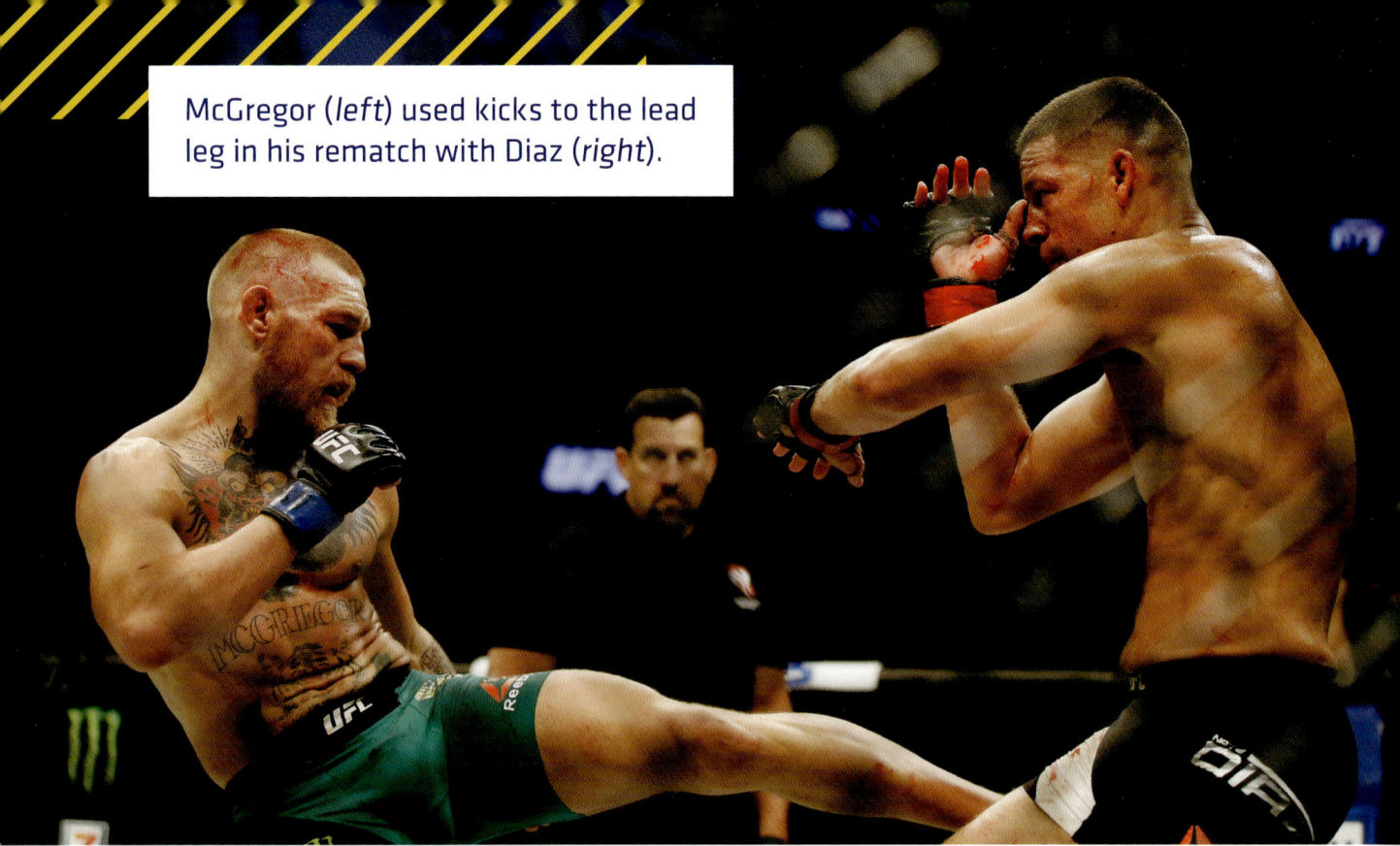

McGregor (*left*) used kicks to the lead leg in his rematch with Diaz (*right*).

training, coaches, and supporters. There have been some famous fights where a clear game plan was effective.

MCGREGOR vs. DIAZ

When McGregor first faced Diaz in March 2016, McGregor was expected to win. Diaz was a replacement for Rafael dos Anjos, who was going to fight McGregor until he broke his foot. Diaz only had 11 days to prepare for the fight. So, few people thought Diaz could win against McGregor, who was undefeated in the UFC and had just won the featherweight title a few months earlier. However, in the second round, Diaz managed to get McGregor in a rear naked choke, forcing McGregor to tap out.

   A rematch was scheduled for August 2016. McGregor was determined not to lose to Diaz again. McGregor and his team watched many recordings of Diaz's fights. They realized that Diaz often stood with most of his weight on his lead leg. They came up with a plan for McGregor to kick Diaz's lead leg to throw him off balance. McGregor practiced leg kicks throughout his training for the second fight.

During the fight, McGregor repeatedly aimed leg kicks at Diaz's lead leg. Not only did this affect Diaz's balance but also his leg was injured during the fight. Neither fighter was able to finish the other, so the fight ended in a judges' decision. The win went to McGregor in a split decision.

KAMARU USMAN vs. JORGE MASVIDAL

In 2020, Kamaru Usman was the UFC welterweight champion and one of the UFC's biggest stars. He was going to defend his title

Usman (*top*) and Masvidal (*bottom*) faced off again in 2021. This time Usman knocked Masvidal out.

against Jorge Masvidal on July 12, 2020. Usman prepared carefully for the fight. He knew his best chance was to take Masvidal to the ground where he could use wrestling moves. Usman's plan worked. He wrestled Masvidal on the ground and also pushed him up against the cage to wear him out. This worked well, as he won every round and retained his belt.

FRANCIS NGANNOU VS. CIRYL GANE

Francis Ngannou is known as possibly the hardest hitter in UFC history. He won the UFC heavyweight championship in 2021, relying heavily on his boxing background. Even though he won a title, many people questioned the strength of his ground game and wrestling skills. In 2018, Ngannou had lost to Stipe Miocic, who out-wrestled him. And Ngannou had barely wrestled in his fights since, so fans didn't know whether he'd improved.

Ngannou's wrestling was tested when he defended his title against Ciryl Gane in January 2022. They spent most of the first two rounds on their feet exchanging blows, and Gane was winning. Then in the third round, Ngannou switched to wrestling. He was able to take Gane down several times and control him on the ground.

Francis Ngannou

It was clear that Ngannou had trained in wrestling to prepare for the match, and his wrestling techniques were greatly improved. He won the fight by unanimous judges' decision. One reason that this game plan worked so well is that it shocked Gane. Gane expected Ngannou to fight standing up with him, so he was caught off-guard when Ngannow switched to wrestling.

Ngannou (top) took Gane (bottom) by surprise with his wrestling skills.

Fighters work with coaches and teammates at MMA gyms.

CHAPTER 6

MMA GYMS

All MMA fighters train at gyms. This is where they connect with the coaches and teammates necessary to becoming successful MMA fighters. There are many MMA gyms all over the world. While every gym offers training in all aspects of MMA, some become known for being strong in specific areas. So, if a fighter has a weakness in their game, they can visit a gym known for expertise in that area to get extra coaching.

FAMOUS MMA GYMS

AMERICAN KICKBOXING ACADEMY (AKA), SAN JOSÉ, CALIFORNIA

AKA is one of the most elite wrestling gyms in the world, not just in America. A number of high-level fighters have traveled to AKA to improve their wrestling skills, learn the fundamentals, and become more confident with their grappling.

Cain Velasquez

Former UFC world champions Daniel Cormier, Khabib Nurmagomedov, and Cain Velasquez all trained at AKA. These fighters have shown some of the best wrestling the UFC has ever seen. Cormier is a former Olympian in freestyle wrestling, Nurmagomedov is known as one of the best grapplers in MMA history, and Velasquez was a wrestling-focused heavyweight. Other MMA fighters who represent AKA include Islam Makhachev, Jon Fitch, Luke Rockhold, and BJ Penn, all of whom have held titles or are title contenders.

Daniel Cormier

AMERICAN TOP TEAM (ATT), COCONUT CREEK, FLORIDA

Regarded as one of the best gyms in the United States, ATT has produced many world champions in a number of different organizations. ATT is seen as an MMA gym that provides elite training in all aspects of MMA, which is one reason they have so many high-level fighters. World champions Adriano Moraes, Yaroslav Amosov, and Kyoji Horiguchi are all ATT fighters. Some of the top names in the UFC who have trained at ATT include Amanda Nunes, Dustin Poirier, Jorge Masvidal, and Joanna Jędrzejczyk.

Joanna Jędrzejczyk

Kyoji Horiguchi

Alexander Volkanovski (*left*) in a 2019 fight against José Aldo (*right*)

Israel Adesanya

CITY KICKBOXING, AUCKLAND, NEW ZEALAND

Founded in 2007, City Kickboxing is a relatively new gym. Two of their fighters, Israel Adesanya and Alexander Volkanovski, became world champions, which brought attention to the gym. It is now regarded as one of the top gyms in the world, known for producing some of the best kickboxers in the world.

XTREME COUTURE MIXED MARTIAL ARTS, LAS VEGAS, NEVADA

Founded by former UFC champion Randy Couture, Xtreme Couture boasts a huge roster of high-level MMA athletes. Its Las Vegas facility is one of the biggest in the United States, and many fighters flock to the gym. It's where Francis Ngannou went to improve his wrestling skills before his fight with Ciryl Gane. Miesha Tate, Vinny Magalhaes, and Kevin Lee are some of the most famous fighters who have trained out of Xtreme Couture.

NOVA UNIÃO, RIO DE JANEIRO, BRAZIL

Nova União is one of the oldest MMA gyms

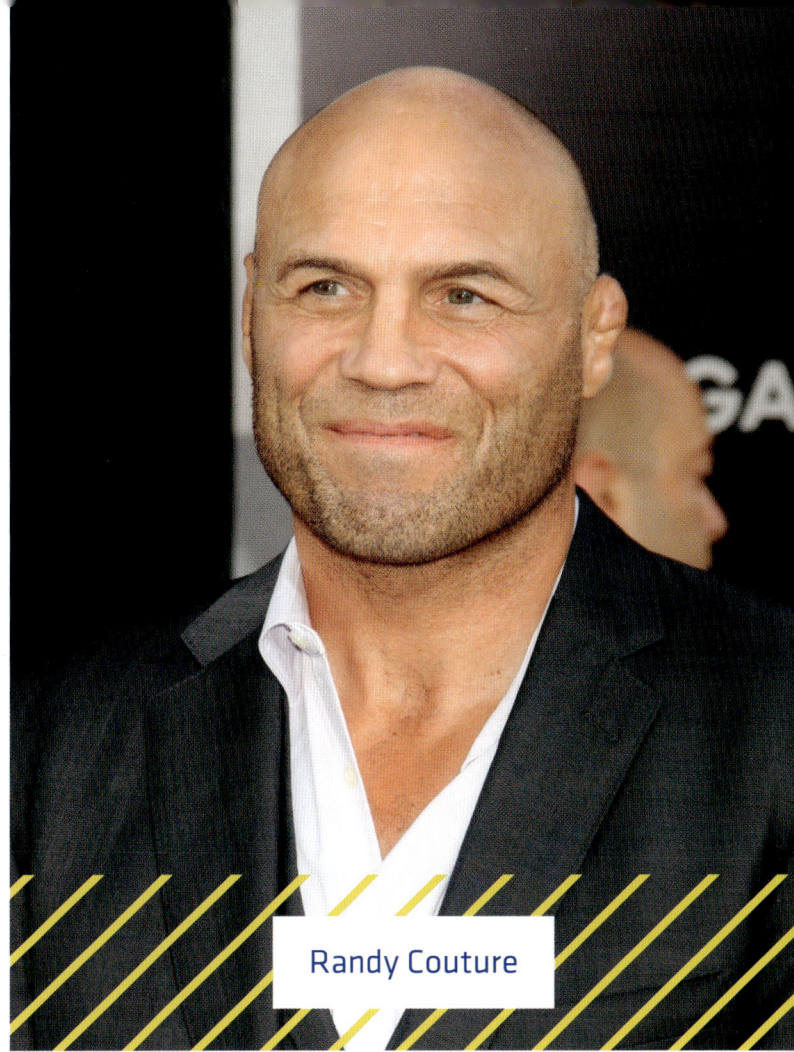

Randy Couture

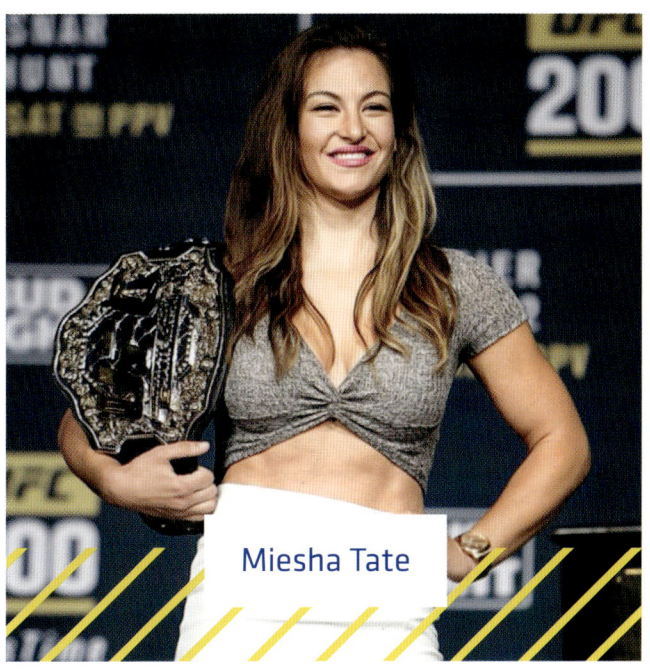

Miesha Tate

José Aldo

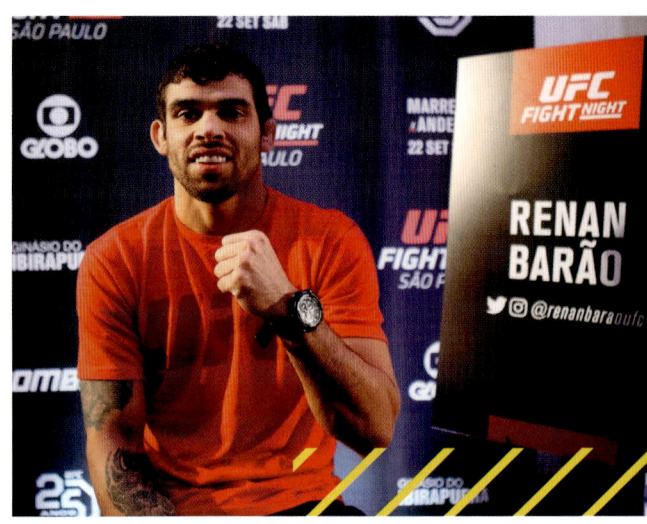

Renan Barão

and Brazil's premier gym, with world-renowned coach André Pederneiras. Nova União rose to fame along with two of its fighters, José Aldo and Renan Barão, who became UFC champions. Nova União is still producing top fighters to this day.

JACKSON WINK MMA ACADEMY, ALBUQUERQUE, NEW MEXICO

Jackson Wink was one of the first gyms to hit the mainstream. It has produced multiple world champions. These include Jon Jones, longtime UFC light heavyweight champion; Holly Holm, the first woman to beat Ronda Rousey; and Carlos Condit, a former World

Jon Jones

Extreme Cagefighting title holder. Jackson Wink is still at the top of the game.

TREVOR WITTMAN, WHEAT RIDGE, COLORADO

Regarded as one of the best coaches in the game, Wittman has been working with fighters in the Denver area since 1998. He has helped established UFC fighters improve their game. Notable clients include

Holly Holm

Trevor Wittman (*left*) trains fighter Nate Marquardt (*right*).

Justin Gaethje

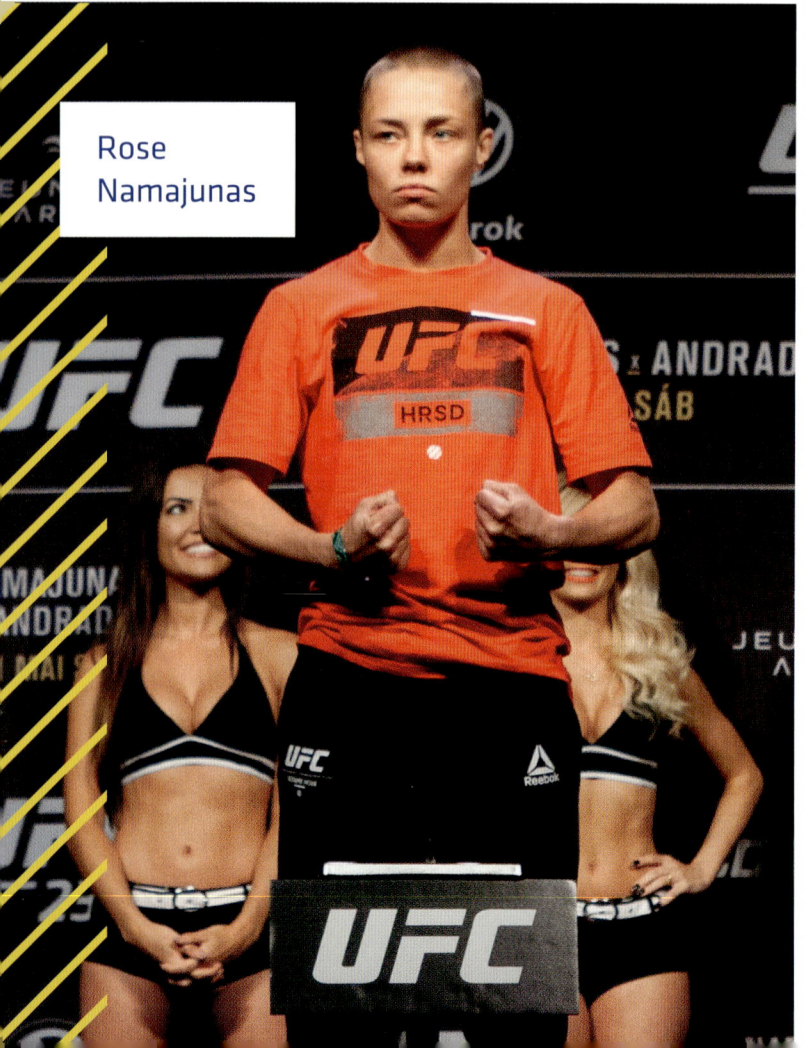

Rose Namajunas

Kamaru Usman, UFC welterweight champion; Rose Namajunas, UFC strawweight champion; and Justin Gaethje, former UFC interim lightweight champion. Wittman won coach of the year in 2021, proving how good he is.

Robbie Lawler is among Kill Cliff's fighters.

KILL CLIFF FC, DEERFIELD BEACH, FLORIDA

Formerly called Sanford MMA and Hard Knocks 365, Kill Cliff and its head coach, Henri Hooft, are well regarded in MMA as having some of the most solid game plans heading into fights. Its notable fighters include UFC welterweight champion Kamaru Usman and three-time world champion Gilbert Burns.

FIGHTIN' WORDS

Here are some common terms used in MMA.

FIGHT CARD // a program or list of the matches during an MMA event. The card usually has one or two headline, or main, matches plus several warm-up, or preliminary, matches.

GRAPPLE // to fight using holds and wrestling moves rather than punches or kicks.

KNOCKOUT (KO) // when one fighter has been knocked down and is unable to get up and resume fighting within a specified time.

ROUND // one of the periods of time a fight is divided into. MMA fights have three or five five-minute rounds with a one-minute rest between each round.

STRIKE // a blow delivered to an opponent while standing. A strike can be made by a fist, knee, elbow, or foot.

SUBMISSION // when a fighter wins by grabbing their opponent in a painful hold that they can't break free of, so that they are forced to give up.

TAKEDOWN // a move that forces or knocks an opponent to the ground.

TAP OUT // when a fighter taps the mat with their hand to indicate that they want to give up.

TECHNICAL KNOCKOUT (TKO) // when a fight referee stops a match because one of the fighters is too injured to continue.

Rafael Cordeiro

KINGS MMA, HUNTINGTON BEACH, CALIFORNIA

Kings MMA head coach Rafael Cordeiro got his start as an instructor at the Brazilian MMA gym Chute Boxe Academy. Cordeiro is famous for his striking expertise, passing on that knowledge to his fighters.

In 2019, while champion Robert Whittaker was out with an injury, Israel Adesanya (*right*) defeated Kelvin Gastelum (*left*) for the interim middleweight belt.

INTERIM CHAMPION

In a title fight, the champion defends their title against a challenger. If the champion has to withdraw due to injury and is replaced by another fighter, the winner of the fight is called the interim champion. When the champion is able to fight again, they will face the interim champion and whoever wins will be the champion. This is referred to as unifying the championship.

MMA ALL-STAR
VALENTINA SHEVCHENKO

Valentina Shevchenko was born in Kyrgyzstan in 1988, when it was part of the Soviet Union. She began training in taekwondo at age five. As she grew older, she switched to Muay Thai kickboxing. Then in 2003, Shevchenko started competing in MMA, winning her first seven fights. In 2007, she moved with her coach to Peru. They became martial arts teachers, and she continued training and competing. Shevchenko joined the UFC in 2015. She has lost twice to Amanda Nunes but has beaten everyone else. In 2018, Shevchenko won the UFC flyweight title, and she has successfully defended it seven times. In June 2022, Shevchenko was the UFC's top-ranked female fighter.

Georges St-Pierre had to withdraw from a title fight in 2011 after suffering a knee injury in training.

CHAPTER 7

WHEN TRAINING GOES WRONG

Even for some of the best athletes in the world, things don't always go according to plan. Key things that could go wrong include injuries, weight misses, and drug test failures. These can happen during training and slow or even end a fighter's career.

Due to the nature of the job, injuries are almost unavoidable. Fighters often get hurt during training camp. Sometimes an injury will force a fighter to withdraw from the fight they were training for. When a fighter withdraws, one of three things can happen. The fight can be canceled, it can be rescheduled for a later date, or the injured fighter can be replaced.

Canceling a fight can cost a promotion money, so when possible, they prefer to replace injured fighters rather than cancel events. This is especially true if the fight is an important one,

Dos Anjos (*pictured*) had to withdraw from a fight with McGregor because he broke his foot during training.

Luke Rockhold

Michael Bisping

such as a title fight. When a fighter needs to be replaced, there are usually a number of other fighters eager for the opportunity. Not only do they get a chance to show their skills in the Octagon but they also show their willingness to step up to help their promotion.

One of the most famous examples of a fighter replacement on short notice was when Nate Diaz replaced lightweight champion Rafael dos Anjos in the fight against Conor McGregor. Another key example occurred in 2016, when UFC middleweight champion Luke Rockhold's opponent had to withdraw and was replaced by Michael Bisping. Rockhold and Bisping had previously met in 2014, and Rockhold won. Rockhold was expected to win the rematch as well. But Bisping surprised everyone by knocking out the champion in less than four minutes. This is considered one of the biggest upsets in MMA history.

50

WEIGHT MISSES

Most fighters are in a specific weight class and have to be a certain weight in order to fight. There is a weigh-in the day before a fight to get each fighter's official weight. Fighters often diet during their training camps to get to their fighting weight for the weigh-in. However, sometimes they miscalculate and end up weighing too much. This is called missing weight. A fighter who misses weight can still fight if their opponent agrees, but they will have to pay a fine. If it's a title fight, they can't win the belt if their weight doesn't match the belt's class.

An example of this was the UFC flyweight title fight held on February 29, 2020. It was between Deiveson Figueiredo and

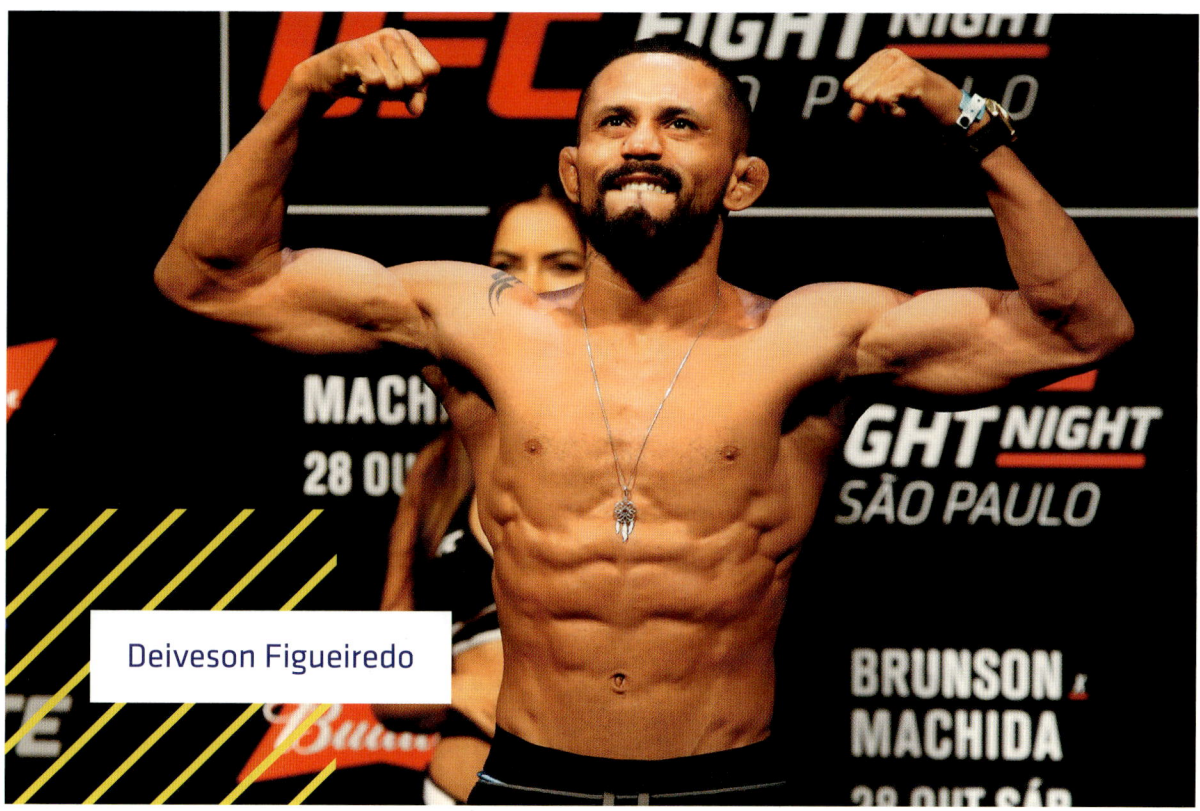

Deiveson Figueiredo

Joseph Benavidez. Figueiredo missed weight, so he was ineligible for the belt and had to give 30 percent of his purse to Benavidez. In the end, Figueiredo won the fight. The two fighters faced each other again a few months later. This time Figueiredo made weight. So, when he won, he was able to win the title.

DRUG FAILURES

In a darker side of the sport, some MMA fighters take performance enhancing drugs (PEDs) to try to get an advantage over their opponents. Some PEDs are taken during training. They help the fighter train for longer, recover faster, and increase their endurance. The United States Anti-Doping Agency (USADA) was established in 2000. This has made it harder for fighters to cheat by taking PEDs. A UFC fighter cannot refuse to take a drug test.

T.J. Dillashaw

Unfortunately, there are plenty of examples of fighters testing positive for PEDs. Well-known examples include T.J. Dillashaw, Jon Jones, and Brock Lesnar. Dillashaw was dropping down from bantamweight to compete for the flyweight title. He held the bantamweight title at the time. Dillashaw lost the flyweight title fight in the first round via knockout. After the fight, it was revealed that he had tested positive for a PED that enhances athletic performance. Dillashaw was suspended from competition for two

Knight holds the record for the biggest weight miss in UFC history.

BIGGEST WEIGHT MISSES

William Knight was scheduled to compete at a maximum of 206 pounds (93.4 kg). But when Knight stepped on the scale at weigh-in, he was 218 pounds (99 kg), a whopping 12 pounds (5.4 kg) over his contracted weight. Amazingly, the fight still went ahead, with Knight having to give up 40 percent of his fight purse. For his next match, Knight moved to the heavyweight class, weighing in at 251 pounds (114 kg). Other infamous weight misses include Mackenzie Dern, who once missed weight by 7 pounds (3.2 kg), and Rafael Alves, who missed weight by 11.5 pounds (5.2 kg) for a 2021 bout. Understandably, both of these fighters had to forfeit a percentage of their purses!

Jones has lost title belts due to his use of banned drugs.

years, stripped of his bantamweight title, and fined.

Many people consider Jones to be one of the best MMA fighters of all time. However, he has failed multiple drug tests throughout his career. In 2016 and 2017, Jones failed tests and was stripped of his light heavyweight title twice. He then produced an abnormality in a drug test in 2018, leading to the entire card being moved from Las Vegas to Los Angeles on a week's notice because of different rules for PED tests.

Lesnar, the former World Wrestling Entertainment (WWE) champion and UFC heavyweight champion, was one of the biggest names in MMA. He returned after five years away from the sport for the historic UFC 200. Lesnar defeated Mark Hunt via unanimous decision that night, but he failed two drug tests and was consequently suspended for a year and fined $250,000. Lesnar's win was turned into a no contest, and he hasn't competed in MMA since.

Brock Lesnar

Anderson Silva

Chael Sonnen

LEGACIES TARNISHED BY PED FAILURES

Despite being some of the best athletes in the world, sometimes fighters feel the need to gain an extra edge by taking PEDs. Not only is this against the rules of the sport but it also tarnishes the legacy of the fighters who do this and are caught. Legendary longtime middleweight champion Anderson Silva tested positive for anabolic steroids as well as testosterone after his 2015 bout with Nick Diaz. Similarly, a former foe of Silva, Chael Sonnen is well-known for using drugs throughout his MMA career. A multiple-time UFC title challenger, Sonnen admitted to taking testosterone to get an edge in his fight against Silva. Sonnen has failed two drug tests during his career, which has tarnished his legacy.

In 2019, the UFC Apex opened near the UFC Performance Institute. It is a large production facility that hosts live events as well as recorded shows.

CHAPTER 8

THE FUTURE OF MMA TRAINING

As MMA continues to evolve, it is inevitable that training methods will change and improve. New technologies, new innovations, and new ideas will shape the MMA of the future. A big part of it will be training.

Knowledge of nutrition, recovery, and training methods will all remain key. However, the way that fighters gain this knowledge and training will likely change. Since the 2017 opening of the UFC Performance Institute (PI) in Las Vegas, fighters' preparation has been greatly enhanced. The PI focuses on getting athletes to compete at their highest potential and offers a number of services to help athletes. These services promote fighter health, well-being, and injury reduction as well as aiding recovery.

The PI has 3D-motion capture capabilities that fighters can use when training. This means

McGregor demonstrates the equipment at the UFC Performance Institute.

that coaches and fighters can get real-time analysis and instant feedback on techniques and other aspects of training. There is also a hypoxic laboratory, which simulates altitude training. This can benefit fighters by helping them improve endurance, speed, and recovery. It also helps accelerate rehabilitation following injury. Other promotions will likely take inspiration from what the UFC is doing with its PI and provide their athletes with similar facilities in order to get the best out of their fighters.

In recent years, an emphasis has been put on recovery, nutrition, and physical and mental health during training. Gone are the days when fighters would routinely train hard and then go out for a few beers with their team. The value of sleep and nutrition in recovery has been brought to the forefront of athletes' minds. Training cannot be done effectively if an athlete hasn't recovered from their training session the day before. Athletes must recover effectively between training sessions. The training itself may not change much in the near future. Fighters will continue to improve their skills through striking pads and heavy bags and through sparring and fight simulation.

Athletes are recognizing the importance of sleep for effective training.

There is a chance fighters could incorporate virtual reality into their training. This would allow fighters to experience fight situations from their gym. This could potentially aid in a fighter being able to handle their nerves more effectively. Training, like fighting itself, will continue to evolve and improve over time, leading to exciting fights for fans.

TIMELINE

The Gracie family develops Brazilian jiu-jitsu.
1920s

The UFC introduces weight classes.
1997

The United States Anti-Doping Agency (USADA) is established.
2000

Georges St-Pierre withdraws from a title fight due to a knee injury.
2011

1993
The UFC is established.

1998
Trevor Wittman begins training fighters in Colorado.

2007
The training center City Kickboxing is founded in New Zealand.

2015
Conor McGregor defeats Chad Mendes to win a UFC interim championship.

McGregor faces Nate Diaz twice, losing the first fight and winning the second.
2016

Valentina Shevchenko wins the UFC flyweight title.
2018

Francis Ngannou wins the heavyweight championship.
2021

2017
The UFC Performance Institute opens in Las Vegas.

2019
The UFC Apex opens.

2022
Francis Ngannou successfully defends his title against Ciryl Gane.

GLOSSARY

anabolic steroid—a hormone used to help tissue growth that is sometimes abused by athletes to increase muscle size and strength despite possible harmful effects.

consistently—in a way that continues to develop or happen in the same way.

elite—belonging to a group that is considered superior.

enhance—to improve or intensify something.

footwork—the skill with which the feet are moved.

gi—the traditional robe worn by people who practice martial arts such as judo and karate.

headliner—the most important fight at an MMA event. It is held last and is often a title fight.

hone—to improve or perfect something.

hype—to create excitement about something through promotional publicity.

incorporate—to include or work into.

inevitable—definitely going to happen; unavoidable.

infamous—having a bad reputation.

interim—the period of time between two events.

legacy—something important or meaningful handed down from previous generations or from the past.

mainstream—the ideas, attitudes, activities, or trends that are regarded as normal or dominant in society.

notorious—having a widely known and usually negative reputation.

nutrition—the foods needed for health and growth.

potential—something that can occur or be achieved in the future.

premier—first in rank, position, or importance.

promotion—an organization or company that organizes MMA fights and tournaments.

roster—a list of members.

showcase—to exhibit something to try to get others to like it.

supplement—something that adds on to or completes something else, such as products that add nutrients beyond those already in a person's diet.

tarnish—to make something less respectable or admirable.

technique—a method or style in which something is done.

ONLINE RESOURCES

Booklinks
NONFICTION NETWORK
FREE! ONLINE NONFICTION RESOURCES

To learn more about MMA training, please visit **abdobooklinks.com** or scan this QR code. These links are routinely monitored and updated to provide the most current information available.

INDEX

Adesanya, Israel, 40
Aldo, José, 5–7, 42
Alves, Rafael, 53
American Kickboxing Academy (AKA), 37–38
American Top Team (ATT), 39
Amosov, Yaroslav, 39
Anjos, Rafael dos, 32, 50

Barão, Renan, 42
Benavidez, Joseph, 52
Bisping, Michael, 50
boxing, 9, 11, 34
Brazil, 10, 14, 41–42, 46
Brazilian jiu-jitsu (BJJ), 10
Burns, Gilbert, 45

California, 37, 46, 54
cardiovascular (cardio) training, 23–24
Chute Boxe Academy, 14, 46
City Kickboxing, 40
coaching, 12–13, 19, 26, 29, 32, 37, 42–47, 58
Condit, Carlos, 42
Cordeiro, Rafael, 46
Cormier, Daniel, 38
Couture, Randy, 41

Dern, Mackenzie, 53
Diaz, Nate, 19, 32–33, 50, 55
Dillashaw, T.J., 52, 54

fighting styles, 6, 9, 13, 17, 19, 31
Figueiredo, Deiveson, 51–52
Fitch, Jon, 38
fitness, 23–26, 29, 57–58

Gaethje, Justin, 44
game plan, 6, 9, 17, 19, 31–33, 35, 45
Gane, Ciryl, 34–35, 41
Gracie family, 10
gyms, 14, 18, 37–46, 59

Holm, Holly, 42
Hooft, Henri, 45

Horiguchi, Kyoji, 39
Hunt, Mark, 54

injury, 5, 14, 21, 24, 29, 33, 49, 57–58

Jackson Wink MMA Academy, 42–43
Jędrzejczyk, Joanna, 39
jiu-jitsu, 9–10
Jones, Jon, 42, 52, 54
judo, 9–10

kickboxing, 9, 11, 18, 40
Kill Cliff FC, 45
Kings MMA, 46
Knight, William, 53

Lawler, Robbie, 21
Lee, Kevin, 41
Lesnar, Brock, 52, 54

Magalhaes, Vinny, 41
Makhachev, Islam, 38
Masvidal, Jorge, 33–34, 39
McGregor, Conor, 5–7, 9, 14, 19, 32–33, 50
Mendes, Chad, 5–7
Miocic, Stipe, 34
missing weight, 49, 51–53
Moraes, Adriano, 39
Muay Thai, 6, 9, 11, 47

Namajunas, Rose, 44
Nevada, 41, 54, 57
Ngannou, Francis, 34–35, 41
Nova União, 41–42
Nunes, Amanda, 39, 47
Nurmagomedov, Khabib, 38
nutrition, 27–29, 51, 57–59

Octagon, 5, 17, 50
Olympic Games, 38

Pederneiras, André, 42
Penn, BJ, 38
performance enhancing drugs (PEDs), 49, 52, 54–55

Poirier, Dustin, 39

recovery, 28–29, 57–59
Rockhold, Luke, 38, 50
Rousey, Ronda, 42

Shevchenko, Valentina, 47
Silva, Anderson, 55
Sonnen, Chael, 55
sparring, 12–14, 17–19, 21, 59
strength training, 24–26

taekwondo, 47
Tate, Miesha, 41
technology, 28, 57–59
training camps, 17, 19, 24, 27, 31, 49, 51

UFC Performance Institute (PI), 57–58
Ultimate Fighting Championship (UFC), 5, 13, 15, 21, 24, 26, 32–34, 38–45, 47, 50–55, 58
United States, 11, 37, 39, 41
United States Anti-Doping Agency (USADA), 52
Usman, Kamaru, 24, 33–34, 44–45

Velasquez, Cain, 38
Volkanovski, Alexander, 40

Wallace, Conor, 19
weigh-ins, 26, 51
weight classes, 5, 7, 21, 24, 26–27, 32–34, 38, 42, 44–45, 47, 50–55
weight cutting, 26–28
Wittman, Trevor, 43–44
World Extreme Cagefighting, 42–43
World Wrestling Entertainment (WWE), 54
wrestling, 6, 9–11, 18, 34–35, 37–38, 41

Xtreme Couture Mixed Martial Arts, 41